CONTENTS

INTRODUCTION — 9

CHAPTER 1:
SETTING THE STAGE FOR SUCCESS — 15

CHAPTER 2:
BUILDING A STRONG FOUNDATION:
BUSINESS ESSENTIALS — 27

CHAPTER 3:
MASTERING MARKETING:
ATTRACTING THE RIGHT CLIENTS — 41

CHAPTER 4:
SALES AND CLIENT ACQUISITION:
CONVERTING LEADS INTO CLIENTS — 55

CHAPTER 5:
TEAM BUILDING AND LEADERSHIP:
CREATING A HIGH-PERFORMANCE CULTURE — 69

CHAPTER 6:
ENHANCING CLIENT EXPERIENCE:
TURNING CLIENTS INTO ADVOCATES   79

CHAPTER 7:
SCALING YOUR PRACTICE:
STRATEGIES FOR SUSTAINABLE GROWTH   89

CHAPTER 8:
FINANCIAL MANAGEMENT:
BUILDING A STRONG FINANCIAL FOUNDATION   95

CHAPTER 9:
NAVIGATING CHALLENGES:
ENSURING RESILIENCE AND ADAPTABILITY   105

CHAPTER 10:
NETWORKING AND COLLABORATION:
BUILDING RELATIONSHIPS FOR GROWTH   113

CONCLUSION:
THE ROAD TO ACCELERATED GROWTH   121

ABOUT BAMBIZ   125

ABOUT THE AUTHORS   129

Rave Reviews from Elder Law & Estate Planning Firms on the Strategies in This Book

"Thanks to Bambiz and their incredibly caring team, I am now living my dream of conducting estate planning workshops in front of packed crowds. Bambiz excels not only in workshop marketing but also in providing unwavering support every step of the way. Their seamless automations and integration with my software have significantly reduced stress for my team. If you are an Estate Planning attorney, don't hesitate — Bambiz is the team you need."
— *Angela Decoteau (Louisiana)*

"What a shift! I had been working with another social media company for promoting in-person events and just assumed that low attendance and non-qualified leads were normal. Nope — Bambiz turned all that around and was able to fill a room with qualified leads at my last event. Highly recommend!"
— *Erica Endyke (California)*

"Jim Blake is a hard working and very talented marketing professional. Jim's marketing ideas and skills have helped my firm share our message and mission with our ideal clients. This has allowed us to grow. I highly recommend Jim Blake and Bambiz for your marketing needs because he can help you too!"
— *Patrick Kelleher (Massachusetts)*

"Jim and his entire team are top notch! Jim and his team helped me fill estate planning and elder law workshops through online marketing consistently. They go above and beyond and well exceeded my expectations with their amazing customer service and their ability to fill workshop rooms. Amazing!"
— Jeffery Bellomo (Pennsylvania)

"Working with the team at Bambiz has been nothing short of a pleasure! They are efficient, responsive, and extremely knowledgeable [...] I can't thank them enough for everything they have done for my business."
— Heidi Friedman (Florida)

"Jim is top shelf. His professionalism, flexibility, and excellent results for us in the workshop arena of Elder Law have been exceptional. His system is very turnkey, and our firm has been very pleased with our ROI using Bambiz. Highly recommend!"
— Jonathan Johnson (California)

Unlock Exclusive Growth Tools

The journey to building a 7-figure law firm on your terms doesn't stop with this book. We've created a collection of bonus materials to help you accelerate your firm's growth even further.

By scanning the QR code below, you'll access exclusive resources, including advanced growth strategies, marketing templates, and step-by-step video guides tailored to estate planning and elder law attorneys. These tools are regularly updated to ensure you continue to have the latest insights and resources to scale your practice.

https://bambiz.net/accelerated-growth-bonus

INTRODUCTION

Imagine this: Your estate planning and elder law firm is not just surviving — but *thriving*. The clients you once chased after now seek you out, referrals are flowing in, and your practice is no longer just a source of income but a powerhouse of impact and influence.

What if, within the next year, you could break through the barriers that have held you back and achieve what so many only dream of — a million-dollar practice?

This isn't a pipe dream. It's the reality we've facilitated time and again with firms that were once in your shoes.

Over the years at Bambiz, we — Jim Blake and Jason Navarro — have had the privilege of working closely with thousands of attorneys across the United States. From solo practitioners to some of the country's largest, most successful firms, we've seen firsthand what it takes to turn a struggling practice into a thriving, million-dollar business — and now, we're here to share those insights with you.

Why This Book?

This book isn't just another business manual filled with generic advice. It's a roadmap built from the trenches of real-world experience in the industry. We've distilled everything we've learned — from our own journeys, from the thousands of client conversations and successes we've had, and from the obstacles we've helped our clients overcome. Then, we put it into a quick read that's straightforward, actionable, and deeply practical for those in elder law and estate planning.

As part of the **Bambiz Rapid Growth Series**, this book is designed to deliver *big results* in the shortest time possible. We focus on providing high-level tactics that you can start implementing right away, helping you make small, strategic changes that lead to significant, sustainable growth. These books are quick reads, perfect for busy professionals who need practical, no-nonsense advice to kickstart their growth journey.

When we talk about growth, we're not just focused on financial rewards. Reaching the million-dollar mark is about more than just numbers. It's about having the freedom to choose cases that ignite your passion, investing in resources that elevate your practice, and building a legacy that endures.

Our Journey to Yours

We've walked this path alongside countless firms, and each one started where you are now — facing the same challenges and ultimately questioning whether real growth is even possible in such a competitive landscape.

As we've gone, we've seen firms that were on the brink of closure turn things around and hit their first million in revenue within a year. We've watched solo practitioners expand into multi-office practices that dominate their markets. And we've guided established firms through the complexities of scaling, helping them double or even triple their revenues.

That's the kind of transformation this quick-read book will offer you — facilitated through a clear, actionable plan to take your firm from where it is now to where you've always wanted it to be.

What You'll Discover

In this book, we'll share the exact strategies that have worked for other successful firms — including what they did, how they did it, and why it worked.

These steps include tasks that help you:

Build a Strong Foundation: As you read, you'll learn how to craft a unique value proposition that resonates with your ideal clients, streamlines your operations for maximum efficiency, and establishes a financial plan that supports sustainable growth.

Mastering Marketing: We'll also show you how to stand out in the world of elder law and estate planning, creating and using your brand identity as a vehicle. After you define your identity, we'll show you how to leverage digital marketing to attract the right clients and build a referral network that keeps your pipeline full.

Refining the Client Experience: Client satisfaction is more than just good service; it's the key to long-term success. In this book, we'll explore how to create a client-centric culture that exceeds the expectations of all parties involved. From optimizing your client intake process to enhancing every touchpoint, you'll learn how to turn satisfied clients into raving fans who refer your firm to others.

Scaling Your Operations: Growth brings new challenges, but with the right strategies, you can scale without losing what makes your firm unique. We'll guide you through the process of expanding your services, opening new locations, and building a team that shares your vision and commitment to excellence.

Ready to Get Started?

The journey ahead is filled with opportunities for growth and transformation. With this book as your roadmap, you'll have the tools to navigate the challenges and seize the opportunities that come your way.

After all, success in this industry isn't about luck — it's about strategy, mindset, and action. And we're here to show you exactly how to achieve it.

So, let's get started.

Disclaimer: *The strategies and insights shared in this book are based on our experiences working with law firms over the years. While we've seen these approaches help firms achieve significant growth, including reaching and exceeding the million-dollar revenue mark, we cannot guarantee any specific financial outcomes. Your success will depend on various factors, including the effort you put in, your market, and individual circumstances. By continuing to read this book, you acknowledge that no income claims are being made and that results may vary.*

Remember — just like anything in life, the more work you put in, the better your chances of achieving your goals. We're here to provide guidance, but the ultimate outcome is in your hands.

CHAPTER 1:
SETTING THE STAGE FOR SUCCESS

Why This Book Matters

The legal marketplace is complex, constantly evolving, and filled with both challenges and opportunities. Many small firms find themselves stuck in a cycle, unable to break through the $500,000 revenue ceiling despite their best efforts.

If you find yourself in a similar position, I want to remind you of something — reaching a million dollars in revenue isn't just a distant dream. It's an achievable milestone that can transform your practice and your life.

Consider the story of a small suburban law firm specializing in estate planning. The partners were skilled attorneys but lacked a clear business strategy.

After attending a growth strategies workshop, they implemented key changes, such as streamlining operations, investing in digital marketing, and building a robust referral network. Within two years, their revenue doubled. They had hired additional staff, took on more clients, and, ultimately, delivered better service.

This transformation didn't just improve their financial standing; it also enhanced their work-life balance, allowing them to focus on what they loved — helping clients navigate complex legal issues.

The journey from struggling to thriving is a road well-traveled by those who are willing to embrace change and invest in growth.

This book serves as your guide, providing a roadmap to success that addresses the unique challenges small firms face while highlighting the abundant opportunities in today's legal market.

To define what the path to success looks like, however, it's important to understand the challenges ahead. For example: A significant hurdle for small firms is the lack of resources. Unlike larger firms with extensive marketing budgets and large staff, small practices typically operate with limited personnel and financial constraints. This makes it difficult to invest in essential areas like marketing, technology, and client engagement.

Another common challenge is balancing the practice of law with the demands of running a business. Many attorneys excel in their legal expertise but struggle with the business side of their practice.

In either challenge "case," there is a solution (or several). This book breaks down complex business concepts and solutions into manageable steps, making it easier for you to implement changes without feeling overwhelmed.

Opportunities for growth are abundant for those willing to adapt and innovate. The legal industry is ripe for disruption, and small firms are uniquely positioned to capitalize on this shift. With the rise of digital marketing, automation, and virtual consultations, the barriers to scaling your practice have never been fewer. This ultimately leads to endless potential for success, both for clients and for stakeholders.

As you continue through this book, you'll encounter real-world examples of firms that have successfully scaled their operations and reached the million-dollar mark. These stories are not just meant to inspire—they provide practical lessons that you can apply to your own practice. By learning from those who have walked this path before you, you'll gain valuable insights into what works, what doesn't, and why.

Whether you're just starting out or looking to elevate your practice, the strategies and insights provided here will help you achieve your goals.

The Million-Dollar Mindset

Achieving a million dollars in revenue for your small estate planning and elder law firm isn't just about implementing the right strategies; it's about cultivating the right mindset. This section delves into the mental framework necessary to propel your firm to new heights.

Vision is the cornerstone of any successful endeavor. It's the ability to see beyond the present circumstances and imagine a future where your firm thrives; acting as aNorth Star that guides your decisions and actions.

For example: Consider a small law firm in a rural area with a vision of becoming their region's go-to firm for elder law. Despite the limited market size, they focused on building a reputation for excellence and community involvement. They hosted free seminars, participated in local events, and consistently delivered high-quality service. Over time, their vision became a reality, with steady client and revenue growth.

Determination is what keeps your vision alive. It's the unwavering commitment to your goals, even when you're faced with obstacles. After all — building a million-dollar firm is a marathon, not a sprint. There will be setbacks and moments when giving up seems easier. However, those who succeed persist.

Resilience is another crucial element for mindset success. In the legal profession, where the stakes are often high, resilience can make the difference between success and failure. A resilient mindset allows you to view challenges as growth opportunities rather than insurmountable obstacles.

Adaptability is essential for long-term success. In the legal landscape, remaining adaptable means staying informed about industry trends, being open to new ideas, and remaining willing to pivot when necessary.

Confidence is also a vital component of the million-dollar mindset. Confidence in your abilities, your team, and your vision can inspire trust and attract clients. A growth mindset is essential. This is the belief that your abilities and intelligence can be developed through dedication and hard work. It fosters a love for learning and resilience, which is critical for achieving long-term success. Cultivating a million-dollar mindset involves having a clear vision, unwavering determination, resilience in the face of setbacks, adaptability to changing circumstances, confidence in your abilities, and a commitment to continuous growth. These mental attributes will not only help you navigate the challenges of running a small law firm but also position you for significant growth and success.

As we move forward in this book, keep these principles in mind. They will serve as the foundation upon which you can build a thriving, million-dollar practice.

Understanding Your Starting Point

Before transforming your small estate planning and elder law firm into a million-dollar practice, you have to understand where you currently stand. This process of understanding involves a thorough assessment of your business metrics, identification of your strengths and weaknesses, and the establishment of realistic goals. Understanding your starting point also involves a candid assessment of your firm's culture and values. A positive, client-centric culture can be a significant strength, while a toxic or disorganized environment can hinder growth.

In addition to internal assessments, seeking external feedback can provide valuable insights. Client surveys, online reviews, and feedback from referral partners can highlight where your firm excels and where it falls short.

Knowing your starting point provides a clear baseline against which to measure progress as you go and supports you in making informed decisions.

The first step in understanding your starting point is to assess your current business metrics. These metrics serve as vital signs of your practice, offering insights into its health and performance. Key metrics to track include revenue, profit margins, client acquisition costs, client retention rates, and average case value. Tracking these metrics over time helps you identify trends and areas needing improvement.

While reporting can be tedious, the benefits outweigh the costs. One real-world example of the importance of tracking business metrics comes from a small firm we worked with that initially struggled with profitability. By closely monitoring their financial metrics, they discovered that their client acquisition costs were disproportionately high. This insight prompted them to reevaluate their marketing strategies and focus on more cost-effective methods, such as referral programs and workshop marketing. As a result, they reduced their acquisition costs and significantly improved their profit margins.

Once you assess your metrics, it's time to identify your firm's strengths and weaknesses. A SWOT analysis (or an analysis of your strengths, weaknesses, opportunities, and threats) can be valuable in this regard.

While strengths are likely the easiest to identify, opportunities and threats can be more complex and require a brutally honest view of your firm. Opportunities, in this context, might include emerging trends in the legal industry or regulatory changes that could benefit your practice or untapped markets. Conversely, threats could be increased competition, economic downturns, or changes in client behavior. Identifying both of these factors helps you develop strategies to capitalize on opportunities and mitigate threats.

Setting realistic growth goals is the final step in understanding (and moving from) your starting point. These goals should be SMART, specific, measurable, achievable, relevant, and time-bound (SMART).

For instance, instead of setting a vague goal like "increase revenue," a SMART goal would be "increase revenue by 25% over the next 12 months by expanding our service offerings and improving client retention." Having clear, actionable goals provides direction and motivation for your team.

Knowing where you stand today is the key to charting the path to where you want to be tomorrow. By assessing your current business metrics, identifying strengths and weaknesses, and setting realistic growth goals, you lay the foundation for informed decision-making and strategic planning. This comprehensive understanding of your firm's current state will serve as a roadmap, guiding you toward sustainable growth and success as we continue through this book.

The Roadmap Ahead

Now that we've laid the groundwork by understanding why this book matters, cultivating the right mindset, and assessing your starting point, it's time to look at the roadmap ahead.

This book is designed to be your comprehensive guide to transforming your small estate planning and elder law firm into a million-dollar practice. Each chapter delves into specific strategies and tactics to help you achieve this goal, providing actionable insights and real-world examples to guide your journey.

The journey, however, is a challenging one. It requires careful planning, consistent effort, and a willingness to adapt and learn. This book is structured to take you through each stage of this journey, from building a strong foundation to mastering marketing, sales, and client acquisition to scaling your practice and ensuring long-term success.

In the next chapter, we'll focus on building a strong foundation for your firm. This involves crafting your unique value proposition, streamlining your operations, and understanding the essentials of legal practice management. We'll also delve into financial planning and budgeting, providing tools to manage your firm's finances effectively.

As you embark on this journey, keep in mind that each step builds on the last, creating a momentum that will propel your firm toward the million-dollar mark. The strategies and insights shared in this book are not just about achieving financial success — they are about building a practice that gives you the freedom to choose your path, the ability to make a meaningful impact, and the satisfaction of knowing that you've created something lasting and valuable.

Ready? Let's take the next step together.

Chapter 1 Key Takeaways

Jim Blake: Your journey begins with a clear understanding of your current position — assessing your business's metrics, identifying strengths and weaknesses, and setting realistic growth goals.

Growth isn't just about numbers; it's about cultivating the right mindset. Vision, determination, resilience, and adaptability are the cornerstones of success in this industry.

These attributes will ultimately guide your decisions and actions as you navigate the challenges ahead. Remember, this isn't just a business strategy — it's about building a practice that gives you the freedom, impact, and legacy you've always aspired to.

Keep these principles at the forefront as we move forward, and you'll be well-equipped to achieve your goals.

Jason Navarro: Understanding where your firm stands today is critical to planning where it can go tomorrow. By assessing your current business metrics and identifying areas for improvement, you set the stage for growth.

However, metrics alone won't get you there. It's the mindset — or the vision, determination, resilience, and adaptability — that will drive your firm forward.

A million-dollar firm isn't built overnight; it's the result of consistent, focused efforts and the willingness to adapt to change.

As you delve into the strategies outlined in this book, keep your eyes on the big picture while also honing in on the actionable steps that will lead you to success. The journey is challenging, but with the right mindset and a solid plan, it's absolutely achievable.

CHAPTER 2:
BUILDING A STRONG FOUNDATION: BUSINESS ESSENTIALS

Crafting Your Unique Value Proposition

Having a Unique Value Proposition (UVP) is non-negotiable.

Your UVP is the beacon that sets your firm apart from the rest, clearly communicating the distinct benefits clients can expect when they choose you. Crafting a compelling UVP isn't just about marketing — it's about deeply understanding your target audience, identifying your firm's strengths, and articulating what makes your services truly unique.

We recommend that you start by diving deep into the psyche of your ideal clients. *Who are they? What keeps them up at night?*

For instance, estate planning clients might be worried about protecting their assets, ensuring their wishes are respected, and minimizing tax burdens. Elder law clients could be more focused on long-term care planning, guardianship, and Medicaid eligibility.

Once you understand these needs, you can craft a UVP that speaks directly to them, making your firm the obvious choice.

After you've done your deep dive into the psyche of your prospective clients, it's time to align those needs with what your firm does best — showcasing your firm as the clear, differentiated "better" alternative than the rest.

Start by reflecting on what differentiates your firm. *Is it your unparalleled experience, your innovative approach, or perhaps the personalized attention you provide each client?* Your UVP should directly reflect the strengths you choose.

For example: If your firm has attorneys with specialized certifications in elder law, that's a significant differentiator. Conversely, if you offer personalized services, like home visits for elderly clients or comprehensive estate planning workshops, these can be key elements of your UVP.

Once you've pinpointed your target audience and firm strengths, it's time to distill your summary of information into a clear, concise, and compelling UVP.

Ultimately, your UVP should answer a fundamental question: *"Why should clients choose your firm over others?"* Additionally, it should be a succinct statement or answer that conveys the unique benefits of your services and how they meet the specific needs of your clients.

A strong example of a UVP for an estate planning firm specializing in working blended families would be: "We provide estate planning services tailored to the unique needs of blended families, ensuring that your wishes are honored and your loved ones are protected." This UVP clearly communicates the firm's expertise and the specific benefits clients can expect.

Another example might be a firm offering comprehensive elder law services, including long-term care planning, guardianship, and Medicaid eligibility. Their UVP could be: "Our experienced elder law attorneys provide compassionate and comprehensive legal services to help you navigate the complexities of aging and ensure your peace of mind." This UVP highlights both expertise and the emotional support the firm offers, setting it apart in the elder law market.

Remember — your UVP isn't just a one-off statement. It's a core definition that should be consistently communicated across all your marketing materials and client interactions. This practice not only reinforces your UVP but also builds trust with potential clients.

While consistency is key, it's also important to note that your UVP isn't static. It scales as your firm does. So, as your firm grows and the market evolves, we recommend that you regularly review and refine your UVP to ensure it stays relevant and continues to resonate with your target audience.

A strong UVP doesn't just differentiate your firm; it becomes the foundation upon which your entire practice is built. It guides your marketing efforts, informs your client interactions, and shapes the overall direction of your firm. As we move forward in this book, keep your UVP in mind — it will be a key component of your marketing, sales, and client acquisition strategies.

Streamlining Your Operations

Streamlining your operations doesn't just enhance productivity; it boosts client satisfaction and directly impacts your bottom line. This section explores essential operational strategies, including delegation, automation, and the effective use of technology, all of which are aimed at creating a more efficient and responsive practice.

Let's start with the power of delegation. Many attorneys, particularly in small firms, fall into the trap of trying to do everything themselves. This can lead to burnout and inefficiency, as valuable time is spent on tasks that could be delegated.

If your firm struggles to effectively delegate, it can be helpful to remember that effective delegation isn't just about offloading work; it's about empowering your team to take ownership of their roles and contribute to the firm's overall success.

Automation is another powerful tool for streamlining operations. In today's digital age, numerous software solutions can automate repetitive tasks, allowing your team to focus on higher-value activities.

For example: Client management systems can automate appointment scheduling, reminders, and follow-ups; reducing the administrative burden on your staff. Or, document automation software can also save time by generating standard legal documents with just a few clicks, minimizing errors and ensuring consistency.

The possibilities are endless, especially as the field continues to evolve and advance. These advancements, in addition to adding convenience to your processes, often wind up saving firms money over time.

A real-world example of successful automation that saves both time and fiscal resources comes from a small estate planning firm that implemented a document automation system. Previously, attorneys spent hours drafting wills and trusts from scratch. After adopting automation software, they created templates for common documents, significantly reducing the time spent on paperwork. This not only improved efficiency but also allowed the attorneys to take on more clients, ultimately increasing revenue.

Establishing clear processes and workflows is a critical step when it comes to streamlining operations. Often, this step begins with documenting your firm's processes ensures that everyone on your team understands their roles and responsibilities, leading to greater efficiency and consistency.

For example: creating a standardized client intake process can help ensure that all necessary information is collected upfront, reducing the likelihood of delays and miscommunication later on.

As you begin to document, you'll find that regularly reviewing and refining your operational processes is crucial. As your firm grows, your processes may need to be adjusted to accommodate new challenges and opportunities. Conducting periodic assessments can help identify bottlenecks and areas for improvement.

Additionally, fostering a culture of continuous improvement within your firm is vital for long-term success — both during and after this step. Many businesses benefit from encouraging their teams to share ideas for streamlining operations and recognize their contributions. This collaborative approach not only empowers your staff but also leads to innovative solutions that drive efficiency.

Here is a key reminder: Streamlining operations is not just about cutting costs or improving margins — it's about creating a practice where efficiency and excellence go hand in hand.

By focusing on delegation, automation, effective use of technology, clear processes, and a culture of continuous improvement, you can build a firm that is both responsive and resilient, ready to seize the opportunities that lie ahead.

Legal Practice Management

Effective legal practice management is the backbone of any successful estate planning and elder law firm.

Client intake is the first step in managing your legal practice effectively. A streamlined client intake process ensures that you gather all necessary information upfront, set clear expectations with clients, and identify potential issues early on.

If you're not sure where to start, consider the impact of a thorough client intake process on client satisfaction. Clients typically appreciate clear communication and knowing what to expect from the outset. By providing clients with a detailed overview of the process, timelines, and potential costs during the initial consultation, you set the stage for a positive client experience. This transparency then continues to build trust and reduces the likelihood of misunderstandings later in the case.

Case management is another critical aspect of legal practice management. Effective case management involves tracking deadlines, managing documents, and ensuring that each case progresses smoothly from start to finish. Implementing a case management system can help you stay organized, reduce the risk of missed deadlines, and improve collaboration among your team.

Billing and financial management policies should also be considered (and re-considered) in the context of legal practice management. Implementing a transparent and efficient billing process helps maintain cash flow and ensures that clients understand the value of the services they receive.

A good example of this comes from a firm we worked with that switched to an electronic billing system was able to reduce the time spent on invoicing and improve payment collection. By providing clients with detailed, itemized invoices, the firm also reduced disputes and increased client satisfaction.

Compliance and risk management are essential for protecting your firm from legal and ethical pitfalls. Regularly reviewing your firm's compliance practices and staying updated on industry regulations can help mitigate risks and avoid costly mistakes.

Implementing technology solutions can greatly enhance your firm's practice management capabilities. From cloud-based storage solutions that ensure secure access to documents to legal research tools that provide up-to-date information on the latest regulations, technology can streamline operations and improve efficiency.

Another way to promote efficiency in your firm is to ensure that training and professional development are key focuses at every stage. *Why?* Simply put, ensuring that your team has access to ongoing training and development opportunities helps them stay current with industry trends and enhances their skills. This not only improves the quality of work but also contributes to employee satisfaction and retention.

This investment inevitably leads to a culture shift throughout your firm — promoting feelings and expectations of engagement and accountability. Managers can contribute to this culture of accountability by setting clear expectations, providing regular feedback, and holding team members accountable for their performance. Effective legal practice management is about more than just keeping the lights on — it's about creating a firm that runs like a well-oiled machine, where every process is designed to support your growth objectives. By focusing on client intake, case management, billing, compliance, technology, training, and accountability, you can build a practice that is efficient, responsive, and poised for success.

Financial Planning for Sustainable Growth

Financial planning is a critical component of building a strong foundation for your estate planning and elder law firm. Without a solid financial plan, even the best strategies and intentions can fall short.

Here, we've listed a quick summary of the tasks needed to help you financially plan for your firm.

The first step in financial planning is setting clear, achievable revenue goals. These goals should be based on a thorough understanding of your firm's current financial situation and its growth potential. By breaking this information down into quarterly and monthly projections, you'll be able to track the progress of your firm and make adjustments as needed.

Managing expenses is another key aspect of financial planning. This task involves not only tracking your firm's expenditures, but also identifying areas where you can reduce costs without sacrificing quality. This may be a team effort that's supported by other members of your firm.

While there are other steps to this process, cash flow management should be a top priority; as it's essential for maintaining financial stability. One effective strategy to promote healthy cash flow management is to implement a system for regular invoicing and follow-up on overdue payments.

Once you're financially stable, it's time to set the stage for growth by strategic investments. These investments might involve hiring additional staff, investing in marketing initiatives, or upgrading your technology infrastructure. No matter how you choose to invest, however, we recommend that you balance these investments with your firm's cash flow and revenue goals. This typically looks like conducting a cost-benefit analysis to determine your end ROI.

After you lay a healthy financial foundation, it's time to create evergreen mechanisms to keep it healthy and thriving. Regular financial reviews are typically the best way to do this.. A review in this case typically involves regularly reviewing your financial statements, assessing your progress toward your revenue goals, making adjustments as needed..

Tax season is (nearly) always around the corner. As such, tax planning is another crucial aspect of financial planning. Understanding your firm's tax obligations and taking advantage of tax-saving opportunities can significantly impact your bottom line. While it might seem tedious, this is an investment of resources that's always worth it in the end.

Remember: Financial planning should be aligned with your long-term goals for the firm. Whether you're planning to expand, sell the practice, or pass it on to the next generation, your financial plan should support these goals. This forward-thinking approach ensures your firm's continued success and longevity.

Chapter 2 Key Takeaways

Jim Blake: Your UVP is more than just a marketing tool — it's the essence of what makes your firm unique and why clients should choose you. By deeply understanding your client's needs and aligning them with your firm's strengths, you can craft a UVP that resonates and drives growth.

Once you do that, it's time to optimize your operational efficiency. Streamlining your operations through delegation, automation, and the smart use of technology can significantly enhance productivity and client satisfaction. Effective legal practice management, from client intake to billing, ensures that your firm runs like a well-oiled machine, supporting both day-to-day operations and long-term growth.

And of course, as you do this, remember not to forget financial planning. Setting realistic revenue goals, managing expenses, and maintaining steady cash flow are all vital to your firm's sustainability and success.

As you build upon these foundational elements, know you're setting the stage for a practice that's not just profitable — but truly thriving.

Jason Navarro: Operational efficiency is essential for scaling your practice. It's all about leveraging technology and creating workflows that allow your team to focus on what they do best. Legal practice management is another key area to consider as you go, as it encompasses everything from client intake to compliance. Implementing best practices in these areas will not only improve client satisfaction but also free up time and resources for growth.

CHAPTER 3:
MASTERING MARKETING: ATTRACTING THE RIGHT CLIENTS

The Power of a Strong Brand Identity

Your brand is the face of your firm, influencing how potential clients perceive you before they even walk through your door (or pick up the phone).

Building a brand that resonates with your target audience goes beyond making a logo or a catchy tagline; it's about creating an emotional connection and consistently delivering on your promises. The best way to start this process is to create a brand identity.

Your brand identity will set you apart from competitors, build trust, and communicate the essence of your firm's values and services — all with the goals of growing your firm and creating lifelong brand advocates.

Start by defining what your firm stands for. *What are the core values that drive your practice? Is it a commitment to client-centric service, a deep expertise in a niche area of law, or a reputation for fierce advocacy?* These values should be the foundation of your brand, informing every decision you make — from the design of your website to the tone of your client communications.

Consider a small elder law firm that successfully differentiated itself in a competitive market by emphasizing its compassionate approach to client care. They recognized that their clients were often facing emotionally challenging situations, such as planning for long-term care or dealing with the legal aspects of aging. By building a brand around empathy, trust, and personal connection, they attracted clients who valued not just legal expertise but also emotional support. Their website, marketing materials, and even the design of their office reflected this brand, creating a cohesive and compelling identity.

Your brand identity should also reflect the unique strengths and expertise of your firm. For instance, if your firm has a track record of success in complex estate planning cases, consider making this a central part of your brand. For example — you could do this by highlighting your experience and the specific benefits you offer, such as your ability to navigate complicated tax laws or craft personalized estate plans that protect clients' assets for future generations. By doing this, you position your firm as the go-to expert in your field.

We do want to reiterate that a strong brand isn't just about what you say — it's also about how you say it. The tone and voice of your brand should be consistent across all touchpoints, whether it's your website, social media, or client interactions.

If your brand is built on being approachable and client-friendly, you might avoid using overly formal or technical language that might alienate your audience. Instead, opt for clear, accessible communication that reassures clients they are in capable and caring hands.

The visual elements of your brand, such as your logo, color scheme, and typography, should also align with your brand's message. These elements aren't just decorative — they're powerful tools that can evoke emotions and reinforce your brand identity.

For example: A firm that wants to convey professionalism and trustworthiness might choose a classic color palette of deep blues and grays, paired with clean, modern typography. On the other hand, a firm that prides itself on being innovative and forward-thinking might opt for bolder colors and more dynamic design elements.

No matter what you choose, know that consistency is key to building a strong brand identity. A consistent brand experience builds trust and loyalty, encouraging clients to refer your firm to others.

Branding is not a one-time effort, however. It's an ongoing process — and likely one that you'll have to repeat again since your brand should evolve with your firm.

We recommend that you regularly review and refine your brand identity to ensure it continues to resonate with your target audience and reflect your firm's growth and achievements. For instance, a firm that initially focused on estate planning for young families might find its client base shifting toward retirees. In this case, rebranding to highlight expertise in retirement planning and elder law could help attract this new audience.

Building a strong brand identity is an investment in your firm's future. As we move through this chapter, we'll explore how to leverage your new brand as an investment in various other marketing strategies — from digital marketing to community engagement — ensuring that your firm not only stands out but also thrives.

Digital Marketing:
Reaching Clients Where They Are

In an era where most people turn to the internet for information, a strong online presence is crucial. Digital marketing allows you to meet potential clients where they are — online — and position your firm as the solution to their legal needs. Whether through search engine optimization (SEO), content marketing, social media, or email campaigns, digital marketing offers powerful tools to increase your visibility and attract the right clients.

Imagine a potential client searching online for "estate planning attorney near me." If your firm doesn't appear in the top search results, you're missing out on a significant opportunity. This is where SEO comes into play.

SEO involves optimizing your website and content so that it ranks higher in search engine results, making it easier for potential clients to find you. By targeting relevant keywords, such as "estate planning attorney" or "elder law specialist," and optimizing your website's structure and content, you can improve your search engine rankings and attract more qualified leads.

Content marketing is another essential component of digital marketing. By creating and sharing valuable content, such as blog posts, articles, videos, and infographics, you can establish your firm as an authority in your field and build trust with potential clients.

Remember: Content marketing is not about promoting your services directly; it's about providing useful information that addresses your audience's needs and concerns. For example, a blog post explaining the differences between a will and a trust can educate potential clients and position your firm as a knowledgeable resource.

A real-world example of effective content marketing comes from a firm that regularly publishes articles and videos on topics related to estate planning and elder law. They focused on creating content that answered common client questions, such as *"What happens if I die without a will?"* or *"How can I protect my assets from long-term care costs?"* This approach not only attracted more visitors to their website but also established the firm as a trusted expert, leading to increased inquiries and consultations.

Social media is another powerful tool for connecting with potential clients and building your brand. Platforms like Facebook, LinkedIn, and Instagram allow you to engage with your audience, share content, and showcase your firm's personality. Social media is also a great way to reach a broader audience and drive traffic to your website. Many choose to do this by sharing blog posts, client testimonials, and updates about your firm's community involvement — attracting followers who may eventually become clients.

Email marketing is another effective digital strategy to consider if you're looking to nurture leads and keep your firm top-of-mind in potential and existing clients. By sending regular newsletters or targeted email campaigns, you can share valuable content, announce upcoming events, or offer special promotions. Email marketing also allows you to stay connected with your audience and build long-term relationships that can lead to repeat business and referrals.

In summary, digital marketing is a powerful way to expand your reach and attract the right clients, but it requires consistency and a clear strategy. As you develop your digital marketing plan, we recommend focusing on creating content that resonates with your target audience, optimizing your online presence, and engaging with potential clients through social media and email. As you do this, you'll find that you build a strong online presence that drives business growth and positions your firm as a leader in your field.

Local Marketing: Engaging with Your Community Through Workshops, Webinars, and Beyond

Don't underestimate the power of local marketing — particularly the power of hosting workshops and webinars — to build your brand and attract clients. These workshops and webinars serve a dual purpose: they position you as the go-to in your field, and they also deliver effective calls-to-action (CTAs) to a room full of potential clients who are genuinely interested in your services (and who are in a place to engage with them).

One of the most effective ways to drive traffic to these workshops and webinars is through targeted online ads. These ads allow you to reach your ideal audience with precision, ensuring that your message reaches those most likely to attend. By focusing your ads on local adults who are interested in topics like estate planning, you can fill your events with engaged and qualified prospects, maximizing the impact of your efforts.

Consider the impact of a small firm that built its reputation by regularly hosting workshops on estate planning at a local community center. By consistently addressing critical issues like asset protection and avoiding probate, they not only educated their audience but also created a steady stream of new clients. The firm's commitment to community education demonstrated their genuine concern for the well-being of their neighbors, which in turn fostered strong client relationships.

As you grow, you'll find that forming partnerships with local businesses can further enhance your workshops and webinars. Collaborating with financial planners, insurance agents, or local senior centers allows you to co-host events that provide comprehensive value to attendees and may increase your chances of a conversion. For example — partnering with a financial planner to discuss retirement and estate planning can draw a larger, more engaged audience.

While workshops and webinars are key to your local marketing efforts, there are additional strategies that can further solidify your presence in the community, which we've included below:

Participating in Community Events: Many firms choose to sponsor or participate in local charity runs, business expos, or festivals. These events not only increase your firm's visibility but also demonstrate your commitment to the community, reinforcing your image as a caring and engaged business.

Leveraging Local Media: Firm leaders may choose to write articles for the local newspaper, appear on a local radio show, or get featured in community magazines to establish themselves in a community of prospective clients. This is important to consider as local media coverage can significantly boost your firm's visibility and concurrently establish you as an expert in your field.

Building Strategic Partnerships: As you grow and scale, consider collaborating with local businesses that share your client base. Many choose to do this by forming a partnership with a financial planning firm, which could lead to joint seminars and referral opportunities (which, subsequently, enhance your reach and credibility).

Engaging in Educational Outreach: This step can be as simple as offering to speak at local schools or community centers about the importance of estate planning. Doing so not only educates the public but also positions your firm as a valuable resource — building long-term relationships that convert into clients.

Community involvement through workshops, webinars, and these additional strategies is more than just a marketing tactic — it's a powerful way to build genuine relationships and make a lasting impact. By focusing on activities that align with your firm's values and expertise, you can establish a strong local presence that attracts clients who see the value in your services and are ready to take the next step.

Leveraging Referrals:
Building a Network of Advocates

Referrals are one of the most powerful sources of new business for any law firm. After all — when a client or professional contact refers someone to your firm, they are vouching for your credibility, expertise, and the quality of your services.

Building a strong referral network involves cultivating relationships with clients, colleagues, and other professionals who can advocate for your firm and send business your way.

Building relationships with other professionals is an effective way to generate referrals for many. For example, financial advisors, accountants, and insurance agents often work with clients who need legal services. By forming strong relationships with these professionals and offering to collaborate on client matters, you can create a referral network that benefits everyone involved.

However, forming these connections takes work. That's why it's important to stay top-of-mind with your contacts as you begin to forge these points of contact. This process might involve sending regular updates about your firm's services, sharing relevant legal information, or simply reaching out to check in — and every connection requires a personalized approach.

While forming new relationships in this way can be disconcerting to some, it's important to note that you should never be "afraid" to ask for referrals. If you've provided excellent service to a client, let them know that you'd appreciate them recommending your firm to others. You can also incentivize referrals with a formal referral program, offering discounts or rewards to clients who refer new business to your firm.

Referrals are a powerful way to grow your firm, but they require consistent effort and relationship-building. By providing exceptional service, cultivating professional partnerships, and staying engaged with your network, you can create a steady stream of referrals that drive your firm's growth and success.

Chapter 3 Key Takeaways

Jim Blake: Workshops are the most transformative tool for elder law and estate planning practices. If there's one thing to take away from this book, it's the importance of establishing a consistent schedule of workshops — month after month. These events are the key to not only educating your community but also driving significant growth for your firm.

If you focus on this one strategy and run with it, your firm could be on its way to reaching $1 million or more in revenue, in most cases. *Why?* Because workshops build trust, establish your brand as a local authority, and create a steady stream of clients. They also reinforce your personal brand and its awareness in the community.

Remember, your brand isn't just a logo or tagline — it's how your community perceives you, and workshops are the most powerful way to shape that perception.

Combine this approach with a strong digital presence and effective local marketing, and you'll not only attract new clients, you'll also create lasting relationships that ensure your firm's success.

Jason Navarro: A strong brand identity is the foundation of your marketing efforts. It's what makes your firm memorable and trustworthy in the eyes of potential clients. However, branding alone isn't enough. You also need to ensure that your brand reaches your target audience effectively through digital channels like SEO and content marketing.

While optimizing your online presence makes it easier for clients to find you, it's important not to neglect the local marketing efforts, as well. Participating in community events and forming strategic local partnerships are excellent ways to enhance your visibility and credibility within your community. It also lays the groundwork for a robust referral network, which is essential for sustained growth.

By delivering exceptional service and maintaining strong relationships with your clients and professional contacts, you encourage word-of-mouth referrals that bring in new, high-quality clients. And together, these strategies create a comprehensive marketing plan that drives both immediate and long-term growth for your firm.

CHAPTER 4:
SALES AND CLIENT ACQUISITION: CONVERTING LEADS INTO CLIENTS

The Art of Client Acquisition

Client acquisition is both an art and a science. The end goal is to transform your leads into loyal clients who trust you to handle some of the most significant matters in their lives. The strategies you employ at this stage in an effort to convert prospects into clients will determine the trajectory of your firm's growth over time.

In many ways, the client acquisition process begins long before a potential client steps through your door. It starts with the reputation you've built, the first impression your brand creates, and the confidence that your marketing efforts inspire. When a potential client contacts your firm, they are already forming judgments based on these factors. Your job is to ensure that every interaction from that point forward reinforces their decision to choose your firm.

One of the most effective ways to enhance your client acquisition process is to refine your initial consultation strategy. The initial consultation is your first face-to-face opportunity to demonstrate your expertise and build rapport with the potential client.

Instead of letting your lead drive the call, approach this meeting with a clear strategy: understand the client's needs, showcase your firm's capabilities, and articulate the value you bring to the table.

As you have your meeting, you'll find yourself engaging in another critical component of strategy: proactively managing client expectations.

This is a key step to take from the very first interaction, setting clear expectations about what clients can expect from your services, timelines, and costs. Transparency at this stage not only builds trust but also helps to prevent misunderstandings down the line.

Typically, firms that consistently communicate expectations up front find that clients are more satisfied with the process, even when unexpected issues arise because they feel well-informed and prepared.

Follow-up is another key element of successful client acquisition. After the initial consultation, it's important to maintain momentum and keep the lines of communication open.

Whether it's through a personalized email, a phone call, or a formal proposal, following up shows potential clients that you're proactive and genuinely interested in their case. Note that client acquisition isn't just about closing a deal — it's about starting (and fostering) a long-term relationship with each individual. So, each interaction should be seen as an opportunity to build trust, demonstrate your value, and set the foundation for a lasting partnership.

As we explore further in this chapter, the strategies you use to manage consultations, set expectations, and follow up can make all the difference in converting leads into loyal clients.

Optimizing the Intake Process

As mentioned above, the intake process is the gateway through which potential clients become actual clients. It's where first impressions are solidified, and the groundwork for the entire client relationship is laid.

When a potential client contacts your firm, whether through your website, a phone call, or a referral, they should immediately feel that they are in capable hands.

This begins with having a clear, consistent, and efficient intake procedure that every team member follows.

Technology can play a crucial role in this step, optimizing your intake process on autopilot. Client management systems (CMS) or customer relationship management (CRM) tools can automate many aspects of the intake process, from scheduling appointments to sending confirmation emails and reminders.

Personalization is another key aspect of an effective intake process. While standardization is important, it's equally crucial to personalize the experience for each client. This means taking the time to understand their specific needs and concerns and tailoring your communication accordingly.

As you refine and personalize your processes, consider the role of communication in your current and future intake processes. Clients should feel informed and supported from the moment they first contact your firm. This means that firms are tasked with providing clear instructions on what to expect during the consultation, what documents they need to bring, and how the process will unfold if they wish to remain competitive.

Lastly, the intake process should include an element of pre-qualification. Not every lead will be a good fit for your firm, and it's important to identify this early on to avoid wasting time and resources.

This can be done through a brief pre-consultation questionnaire or an initial phone call that helps you assess whether the client's needs align with your firm's expertise.

An optimized intake process is not static — it should be regularly reviewed and refined to ensure it continues to meet the needs of your clients and your firm. By standardizing procedures, leveraging technology, personalizing the client experience, and ensuring clear communication, you can create an intake process that not only converts leads into clients but also sets the stage for a successful and productive client relationship.

Consultation Techniques:
Building Trust and Closing Deals

The consultation is a pivotal moment in the client acquisition process. It's where potential clients get a firsthand look at your expertise, professionalism, and the value you can bring to their situation.

Ultimately, the way your firm conducts this consultation can make the difference between winning the client's business or losing it to a competitor.

When refining this process, it's important not to overcomplicate the steps involved. The first thing to keep in mind is a single, simple fact: Successful consultations are built on a foundation of trust. Clients need to feel that you genuinely understand their concerns and that you have the expertise to address them effectively. This understanding often begins with intentional research and active listening.

During the consultation, give the client your full attention, listen carefully to their needs, and ask insightful questions demonstrating your understanding of their situation. These two steps show both respect and acknowledgment of the client's needs, preparing them to engage well later on.

The next key element of a successful consultation to consider is providing value upfront. Potential clients should leave the consultation feeling like they've gained something valuable, whether it's a new perspective on their legal issue, a clearer understanding of their options, or practical advice they can act on immediately.

While it may seem like the end of a "stage," note that the way you close the consultation is just as important as how you begin it. We recommend that you summarize the key points discussed, reaffirm your understanding of the client's needs, and outline the next steps in order to prepare them to move to the next stage. This step also reinforces the value you bring and keeps the momentum going.

Once your consult is complete, follow up with the lead to determine the next step in their journey. This could look like a personalized follow-up email or a call to thank the client for their time, reiterate the key points discussed, and outline the next steps.

This step not only keeps the lines of communication open, but also shows the client that you're proactive and attentive to their needs.

Consultations are an opportunity to not only showcase your expertise but also to build trust and start forming a strong client relationship. By focusing on active listening, providing value, being transparent, and following up effectively, you can turn consultations into powerful tools for client acquisition and set the stage for long-term success.

Handling Objections:
Turning Hesitation into Commitment

No matter how well you conduct a consultation, you may still encounter objections from potential clients. These objections can range from concerns about cost to uncertainty about the process or hesitation about moving forward. How you handle these objections can determine whether the client chooses to work with your firm or walks away.

The first step in handling objections is to understand where the client's concerns are coming from. Often, objections are rooted in fear, uncertainty, or a lack of understanding. For example, a client might be concerned about the cost of legal services because they're unsure of the value they'll receive in return. Or, they might hesitate to move forward because they don't fully understand the process.

By identifying the underlying cause of the objection, you can address it more effectively.

One effective technique for handling objections is to acknowledge the client's concerns directly with them, and then provide reassurance. For example: if a client expresses concern about the cost of services, you might acknowledge that legal services can be a significant investment but then explain how your expertise and the outcomes you achieve provide long-term value.

Another strategy is to provide evidence that addresses or negates the client's concerns. This could be in the form of case studies, testimonials, or examples of past successes. For instance, if a client is hesitant because they're unsure if your firm can handle their specific legal issue, you could share a case study that demonstrates your experience and success in a similar case. Maintaining empathy is also a powerful way to handle client objections. While simple, this tone shift shows that you understand the client's concerns and that you're committed to helping them navigate their legal challenges; ultimately building trust and rapport.

Sometimes, objections aren't a sign of a bad process or a firm error. They could simply just be a sign that the client isn't ready to make a decision right away. In these cases, it's important to remain patient and supportive. You might provide the client with additional information or resources they can review at their own pace, and let them know that you're available to answer any further questions. Or, you may set time to follow up with them at a later date.

If a client's objection can't be fully resolved, it's best to be prepared with a range of alternative solutions. These solutions or references will look different across firms, subspecialties, and client types. For example, if a client is concerned about the cost, you might offer flexible payment plans or suggest a phased approach to addressing their legal needs.

Handling objections effectively requires a combination of empathy, communication, and problem-solving skills. By understanding the root of the client's concerns, providing reassurance and evidence, and offering alternative solutions, you can turn hesitation into commitment and secure more clients for your firm.

Follow-Up: Maintaining Momentum and Securing Commitment

The follow-up process is a critical, yet often overlooked, component of client acquisition. It's the bridge between a successful consultation and a signed engagement letter.

Effective follow-up begins immediately after the consultation. A personalized follow-up email or phone call can reinforce the positive impression you made during the meeting and keep the momentum going. In your follow-up, reiterate the key points discussed, address any remaining questions or concerns, and outline the next steps clearly. Remain consistent, and schedule a few different follow-up touchpoints for best results.

It's important to reiterate that personalization also plays a crucial role in successful follow-ups. Clients appreciate when you remember details about their case and show genuine interest in helping them achieve their goals, rather than when firms reply with a template. Always take the time to research and add a little personalization to your outreach attempts.

Timing is another critical factor in the follow-up process. Following up too soon might make clients feel rushed, while waiting too long could result in lost opportunities.

An effective follow up process enables firms to maintain momentum, address any lingering concerns, and ultimately secure the client's commitment to the firm, increasing the potential for conversions and client brand advocacy later on.

Chapter 4 Key Takeaways

Jim Blake: Successful client acquisition begins with a clear, organized approach that builds trust from the first interaction. The initial consultation is a pivotal moment where you demonstrate your expertise, listen to the client's needs, and offer valuable insights that set the foundation for a strong relationship. But the process doesn't end there. An optimized intake process ensures that no detail is overlooked and that clients feel supported from the outset.

As you go, you'll find clients with concerns. Handling these objections with empathy and providing clear, tailored solutions helps turn hesitation into commitment and ultimately, conversion. Firms can boost their chances of a client sign-on by creating and following a consistent,well-executed follow-up process; maintaining momentum and securing the client's business interest.

Each step in this process is an opportunity to build trust, reinforce your value, and ultimately grow your firm's client base.

Jason Navarro: Optimizing the intake process ensures that every potential client feels valued and well-served, setting the stage for a positive client relationship.

When the inevitable objections arise, they should be viewed as opportunities to build trust by addressing concerns with transparency and empathy.

The follow-up process is equally vital to the other two points above, as it keeps potential clients engaged and reinforces your commitment to their case. By being proactive, consistent, and personalized in your follow-ups, you can significantly increase your conversion rates and establish a strong foundation for ongoing client relationships.

CHAPTER 5:
TEAM BUILDING AND LEADERSHIP: CREATING A HIGH-PERFORMANCE CULTURE

The Foundation of a Strong Team

No matter how skilled you are as an attorney, the growth and sustainability of your practice depend on the collective efforts of your team.

What's more? Building a strong team isn't just about hiring talented individuals; it's about creating a cohesive, motivated group that shares a common vision and works together to achieve it. And that can be more difficult than it looks. Let's break it down into a few key points of consideration.

The foundation of a strong team starts with a clear and compelling vision. As the leader, it's your responsibility to articulate this vision in a way that resonates with every member of your team. *What are the core values that drive your firm? What long-term goals are you working toward?*

When your team understands and believes in the firm's mission, they are more likely to feel invested in the work they do and the outcomes they achieve.

Hiring the right people is, of course, a critical component of building a strong team. Beyond skills and experience, however, finding a strong cultural fit is equally important.

As you assemble your team, continue to foster a culture of collaboration and mutual support wherever possible. This process can become overcomplicated; but it's really quite simple: Celebrate successes, whether big or small, and acknowledge the hard work that went into achieving them. This not only boosts morale but also reinforces the behaviors and values you want to see in your team. Additionally, encourage open communication, idea-sharing ideas, questions, and feedback. Your team will take it from there, adding their own unique influence to your budding workplace culture.

Maintaining a core focus on professional development is another way to build and foster a strong team. By investing in the growth and education of your team members, you not only enhance their skills but also show that you value their contributions and are committed to their success.

Lastly, leadership plays a crucial role in shaping and maintaining a strong team. As a leader, your actions set the tone for the entire firm.

Lead by example, demonstrating the servant leadership, values and work ethic you expect from your team. Be approachable, transparent, and supportive, creating an environment where your team feels empowered to do their best work. And above all, remain kind, empathetic, and flexible — inspiring them to do the same.

Building a strong team is an ongoing process that requires attention, care, and commitment. By focusing on a shared vision, hiring for cultural fit, fostering collaboration, investing in professional development, recognizing achievements, and leading by example, you can create a team that not only supports your firm's growth but also drives it forward.

Leadership: Guiding Your Team to Success

As the leader of your firm, your role extends beyond managing day-to-day operations; you're also needed to guide your team toward achieving your collective goals — inspiring them to reach their full potential and creating an environment where everyone feels motivated to contribute.

In addition to this list of tasks, one of the key responsibilities of a leader is to set a clear direction for the firm. This involves not only defining your long-term goals but also breaking them down into actionable steps that your team can follow. When your team understands the bigger picture and how their individual efforts contribute to the firm's success, they are more likely to stay focused and motivated.

Inspiring your team is another essential leadership quality. This goes beyond motivating them to complete tasks — instead, you'll inspire them to take ownership of their work, think creatively, and strive for excellence.

Not sure where to start? Lead your team with passion and enthusiasm. When your team sees that you are genuinely excited about the work you do and the impact you're making, they are more likely to feel the same way.

Empowerment is also a key element of effective leadership. Empowering your team means giving them the autonomy to make decisions, take initiative, and contribute to the firm's success in meaningful ways. This not only enhances their sense of ownership and accountability but also fosters innovation and creativity. Leading through change is another important aspect of leadership. The legal industry is constantly evolving, and it's crucial for leaders to guide their teams through periods of change with confidence and clarity. Whether it's adopting new technology, shifting to a different business model, or navigating regulatory changes, your ability to lead through change can make all the difference in how your team responds.

Accountability is also a fundamental principle of leadership. As a leader, it's important to hold yourself and your team accountable for achieving the firm's goals. This means setting clear expectations, providing the necessary resources and support, and following through on commitments.

Effective leadership is about more than just managing — it's about guiding, inspiring, empowering, and supporting your team. By setting a clear direction, maintaining open communication, leading with passion, empowering your team, navigating change, holding everyone accountable, and fostering a positive work environment, you can lead your firm to new heights of success.

Motivating Your Team: Beyond Financial Incentives

Financial incentives such as bonuses and raises are important. However, they are not the only — or even the most effective — way to motivate your team. True motivation comes from a sense of purpose, personal growth, and the recognition that their work makes a difference. As a leader, it's crucial to tap into these deeper sources of motivation to keep your team engaged and driven.

One of the most powerful motivators that doesn't involve financial incentive is a team member's internal sense of purpose. When your team members understand how their work contributes to the firm's mission and the positive impact it has on clients, they are more likely to feel motivated and committed. This rush directly translates to their quality of work. Professional growth and development are also key motivators. By providing opportunities for your team to learn new skills, take on new challenges, and advance in their careers, you can foster a culture of continuous improvement and achievement.

Recognition and appreciation are fundamental to motivating your team. Regularly acknowledging your team's hard work and accomplishments — whether through formal recognition programs, public praise, or personal thank-you notes — can significantly boost morale and motivation.

Helping your team to maintain healthy work-life balance is another critical factor in motivation. When your team feels that their well-being is valued and that they have the flexibility to balance their work and personal lives, they are more likely to be engaged and productive.

Empowerment and autonomy are also powerful motivators. When team members are given the freedom to make decisions, take ownership of their projects, and contribute to the firm's success in meaningful ways, they are more likely to feel motivated and fulfilled. Finally, fostering a positive work environment is essential for motivation. A supportive, inclusive, and collaborative culture can make a significant difference in how motivated your team feels. While it can feel counterintuitive, it's important to remember that motivation is about more than just financial rewards — it's about creating a work environment where your team feels valued, supported, and inspired to do their best work. By tapping into deeper sources of motivation such as purpose, professional growth, recognition, work-life balance, empowerment, and a positive work environment, you can create a team that is not only motivated but also passionate about driving your firm's success.

Chapter 5 Key Takeaways

Jim Blake: Hiring the right people is essential, but it's equally important to foster a culture of collaboration, professional growth, and mutual support. Leadership plays a pivotal role in guiding your team, setting a clear direction, maintaining open communication, and inspiring your team to reach their full potential.

Leaders have to remember that true motivation goes beyond financial incentives — it's about creating a sense of purpose, providing opportunities for growth, recognizing achievements, and fostering a positive work environment.

By focusing on these key elements, you can build a team that is not only committed to your firm's success but also drives it forward with passion and dedication.

Jason Navarro: Leadership is about more than managing tasks — it's about guiding, inspiring, and empowering your team to achieve great outcomes. Motivating your team requires a multifaceted approach that goes beyond financial rewards.

By fostering a sense of purpose, offering opportunities for professional development, and creating a supportive, inclusive work environment, you can cultivate a team that is not only high-performing but also deeply invested in the firm's mission.

Together, these elements create a culture of excellence that propels your firm toward long-term success.

CHAPTER 6:
ENHANCING CLIENT EXPERIENCE: TURNING CLIENTS INTO ADVOCATES

The Importance of Client Experience

While acquiring new clients is critical, retaining them and turning them into advocates for your firm is equally, if not more, important. A positive client experience not only increases satisfaction and loyalty, but also drives referrals and strengthens your firm's reputation.

Client experience, in this context, encompasses every interaction a client has with your firm, from their first contact through to the resolution of their case and beyond. It's about more than just delivering a successful outcome — it's about how clients feel throughout the entire process. A firm that focuses on providing an exceptional client experience is one that pays attention to both the big picture and the small details, ensuring that clients feel valued, understood, and supported at every step.

One of the key elements of a positive client experience is effective communication. Clients want to feel informed and involved in their case. This means providing regular updates and remaining available to answer questions and address concerns.

This matters more than many might think, as the client experience doesn't end when a case is closed. Following up with clients after their case is resolved can leave a lasting positive impression. For example: A firm that implemented a post-case follow-up process, including a thank-you note and a brief survey found that clients were more likely to refer others to the firm and return for additional services in the future. This simple gesture reinforced the firm's commitment to client satisfaction and helped maintain long-term relationships.

Enhancing the client experience requires a thoughtful, client-centric approach that permeates every aspect of your firm. By focusing on communication, empathy, consistency, and follow-up, you can create a client experience that not only satisfies but delights — turning clients into loyal advocates who contribute to the growth and success of your firm.

Personalization: Tailoring the Experience to Each Client

Personalization is a powerful tool in enhancing the client experience. No two clients are the same, and a one-size-fits-all approach can leave clients feeling like just another case number. By tailoring your services and interactions to the unique needs and preferences of each client, you can create a more meaningful and satisfying experience that sets your firm apart.

Communication is a key area where personalization can make a significant impact. Some clients may prefer detailed explanations and frequent updates, while others might appreciate a more streamlined approach with only essential communications. By asking clients about their preferences and adjusting your communication style accordingly, you can make them feel more comfortable and valued.

Personalization also extends to *how* you deliver your services. For instance, some clients may prefer in-person meetings, while others might find virtual consultations more convenient. When you offer flexible options that cater to each client's preferences, you can enhance their overall experience and make your services more accessible.

Another way to personalize the client experience is by paying attention to the small details that matter to your clients. This could be as simple as remembering important dates, such as birthdays or anniversaries, and sending a personalized note or gift. A firm that we've worked with made a habit of acknowledging clients' milestones and significant life events found that this gesture not only strengthened client relationships but also led to more referrals, as clients felt a deeper connection with the firm.

It's also important to remember that personalization also means being responsive to changes in your clients' needs as the case goes on. By anticipating these needs and shifts and proactively offering tailored solutions, you can ensure that your firm remains relevant and valuable to your clients over time — even if the client is going through a particularly "rough" part of the case. Ultimately, personalization is about making each client feel seen, heard, and understood. By tailoring your services, communication, and interactions to meet the unique needs of each client, you can create a more personalized and meaningful client experience that not only meets but exceeds expectations. This level of care and attention to detail will ultimately set your firm apart, helping turn satisfied clients into loyal advocates.

Leveraging Technology to Enhance Client Experience

Technology plays a critical role in enhancing the client experience, especially in this era of law. From streamlining processes to improving communication, the right technology can make it easier for clients to interact with your firm and access the services they need in a sleek, autonomous way.

One of the most impactful ways to use technology is through client portals. These secure online platforms allow clients to access their case information, communicate with their attorney, upload and download documents, and even make payments — all in one convenient place.

While this can be an up-front investment, it does yield significant ROI — and quickly. A firm that implemented a client portal found that clients appreciated the convenience and transparency it offered. Clients could check the status of their case at any time, reducing the need for frequent phone calls and emails. This not only improved the client experience but also freed up time for the firm's staff to focus on more complex tasks.

Automation is another powerful tool for enhancing the client experience. By automating routine tasks such as appointment scheduling, reminders, and follow-ups, you can ensure that these important touchpoints are handled efficiently and consistently.

Automated reminders and follow-ups also helped keep clients on track, ensuring that deadlines are met, your time is protected, and cases move forward smoothly.

Virtual consultations and meetings have become increasingly popular, particularly in the wake of the COVID-19 pandemic. Offering clients the option to meet virtually can provide greater flexibility and convenience, particularly for those with busy schedules or mobility challenges. It can also act as a vehicle for firm expansion; connecting you to clients in new geographic locations.Document management is another underrepresented area where technology can greatly enhance the client experience. By using cloud-based document management systems, you can make it easier for clients to access, review, and sign important documents from anywhere. This implementation typically speeds up the process of document execution while reducing the risk of errors and delays.

Technology can also be used to gather and analyze client feedback, helping you to continuously improve the client experience. This proactive approach to client satisfaction helps many firms maintain high levels of client loyalty and retention.

Lastly, technology can help you personalize the client experience on a larger scale. CRM systems can track client interactions, preferences, and needs; allowing you to tailor your communication and services more effectively. Leveraging technology to enhance the client experience is about more than just adopting the latest tools — it's about using technology in a way that adds real value to your clients. By integrating technology into your processes, you can create a more efficient, transparent, and personalized experience that sets your firm apart and keeps clients coming back.

Chapter 6 Key Takeaways

Jim Blake: By tailoring your services and interactions to each client's unique needs, you enhance their satisfaction and build stronger relationships.

Leveraging technology to do this can further elevate the client experience, offering convenience, transparency, and efficiency that clients appreciate.

Remember: Client retention strategies are equally important, as maintaining long-term relationships with clients not only drives repeat business but also fuels referrals, strengthening your firm's reputation and growth.

By focusing on communication, empathy, and ongoing engagement, you can turn satisfied clients into loyal advocates who actively contribute to your firm's success.

Jason Navarro: A great client experience begins with effective communication and empathy, ensuring that clients feel heard and understood at every stage. Technology offers powerful tools to streamline these processes, improving communication, and enhancing the overall client experience.

By building and nurturing long-term relationships using the tools available, you not only increase client satisfaction; but also create a network of advocates who are eager to refer others to your firm, driving sustainable growth and success.

CHAPTER 7:
SCALING YOUR PRACTICE: STRATEGIES FOR SUSTAINABLE GROWTH

Expanding Your Service Offerings

One of the most effective ways to scale your practice is by expanding your service offerings. Diversifying the services you provide not only allows you to meet the evolving needs of your clients but also opens up new revenue streams and market opportunities.

However, while this step can offer value, we want to reiterate expanding your services requires careful planning and execution to ensure that the quality of your core offerings remains intact. It's better to scale slowly and strategically than hastily with gaps in your client experience.

Often, the first step in expanding your service offerings is to assess the needs of your existing client base. If you're not sure where to start, ask yourself: *What additional services could you provide that would add value to their experience and address their legal needs more comprehensively?* For example, a firm that initially specialized in estate planning identified a growing demand for elder law services among their clients. By expanding their offerings to include Medicaid planning, long-term care planning, and guardianship services, they were able to better serve their clients while also attracting new business.

This strategic expansion not only increased revenue but also strengthened the firm's reputation as a comprehensive resource for elder law and estate planning.

Another approach to expanding your service offerings is to explore complementary areas of law that align with your firm's existing expertise. As you expand, ensure that you have the necessary resources and expertise to deliver these services effectively. This may involve hiring additional staff, investing in training for your existing team, or partnering with other professionals who can provide the specialized knowledge you need.

Once you've added new services, it's time to market them. As you scale, consider adopting a flexible marketing strategy that continuously communicates changes to both existing clients and potential clients.

Expanding your service offerings is a powerful strategy for scaling your practice, but it requires careful planning, execution, and ongoing evaluation. By understanding your clients' needs, leveraging your firm's expertise, building the right team, and effectively marketing your new services, you can create new growth opportunities and position your firm for continued success.

Chapter 7 Key Takeaways

Jim Blake: Scaling is not just about growing in size; it's about building a resilient, sustainable practice that can thrive in the long term. This begins with adopting a growth mindset, where strategic planning, innovation, and resilience are at the forefront. Expanding your service offerings is a key strategy for growth, but it must be done thoughtfully to ensure that the quality of your core services remains intact.

Once you expand, it's important to focus on streamlining operations through process optimization, automation, and the use of technology; as mentioned in the prior chapter. While it is an investment of time and liquidity, this step is critical to handling increased demand efficiently.

Once you complete this step, it's time to hire. Focus on hiring for both skill and cultural fit, investing in training and development, and building a strong leadership team that can guide your firm toward its long-term goals. By focusing on these elements of scalability, you can grow your practice sustainably and position your firm for continued success.

Jason Navarro: Expanding your team is about more than just adding staff; it's about building a structure that supports growth and fosters a culture of excellence. By hiring strategically, investing in onboarding and training, and developing your leadership team, you can build the capacity needed to support your firm's growth and ensure its long-term success.

The strategies above, when combined, provide a roadmap for scaling your practice in a way that is both sustainable and aligned with your firm's vision for the future.

CHAPTER 8:
FINANCIAL MANAGEMENT: BUILDING A STRONG FINANCIAL FOUNDATION

The Importance of Financial Planning

Financial management is the backbone of any successful law firm; ensuring that your firm has the resources it needs to grow, adapt, and thrive in the long term. Effective financial management allows you to make informed decisions, allocate resources strategically, and navigate challenges with confidence.

As with everything else, we have to start by laying a foundation. The foundation of sound financial management is a comprehensive financial plan.

This plan should encompass all aspects of your firm's finances, from revenue projections and expense management to cash flow planning and investment strategies. This proactive approach allows you to manage your resources more effectively; ensuring that they were well-prepared to meet both expected and unexpected challenges.

One of the key components of financial planning is setting realistic revenue goals. These goals should be based on a thorough analysis of your firm's historical performance, market trends, and growth potential.

As mentioned earlier on in this book, expense management is another critical element of financial planning. Keeping a close eye on your firm's expenses helps you identify areas where you can reduce costs without compromising on quality. This directly affects your ability to set realistic revenue goals.

Investing in your firm's growth is a crucial aspect of financial planning. This might involve hiring additional staff, upgrading your technology, or expanding your service offerings. However, it's important to balance these investments with your firm's overall financial goals.

A firm that carefully plans its investments, conducting cost-benefit analyses and ensuring that every step aligned with their long-term strategy, is able to grow sustainably without overextending itself.

Effective financial management is the cornerstone of a successful and sustainable law firm. By implementing the suggestions offered in this chapter, you can build a strong financial foundation that supports your firm's long-term success. A solid financial foundation is key to achieving your goals and building the million-dollar practice you envision.

Managing Cash Flow: Ensuring Stability and Growth

Cash flow is the lifeblood of any business, and your law firm is no exception. Effective cash flow management ensures that your firm has the financial stability to meet its obligations, invest in growth opportunities, and navigate periods of uncertainty. Without proper cash flow management, even the most successful firms can find themselves in financial trouble.

One of the most important aspects of managing cash flow is understanding the timing of your inflows and outflows. This means having a clear picture of when money is coming into your firm and when it needs to go out. Many do this by creating a detailed cash flow forecast, projecting their income and expenses on a weekly and monthly basis. This allows firms to anticipate and address potential cash flow shortfalls before they became a problem.

Looking to bolster your incoming cash flow? Invoicing practices play a critical role in cash flow management. Prompt and accurate invoicing ensures that your firm gets paid on time, which is essential for maintaining a healthy flow in.

Retainer agreements can also help stabilize cash flow by ensuring that your firm receives payment upfront. This approach also helps manage client expectations and reduces the risk of disputes over billing.

Another strategy for managing cash flow is to build and maintain a financial buffer. Setting aside a portion of your revenue each month to create a cash reserve can provide a cushion during slow periods or in the event of unexpected expenses. Consistently saving a percentage of firm income allows many to create a reserve fund that allows them to weather temporary cash flow challenges without needing to rely on credit or cut back on essential expenses.

Lastly, cash flow management software provide real-time insights into your firm's financial health; helping you make informed decisions and avoid potential cash flow issues. These work to automatically identify trends, and make proactive adjustments to keep cash flow stable.

Managing cash flow is essential for the financial health and growth of your firm. By developing a clear understanding of your inflows and outflows, streamlining invoicing practices, using retainer agreements, building a financial buffer, monitoring expenses, and leveraging technology, you can ensure that your firm remains financially stable and well-positioned for growth.

Budgeting for Growth:
Aligning Resources with Goals

A well-structured budget is a powerful tool for guiding your firm's growth and ensuring that your resources are aligned with your strategic goals.

Budgeting helps you allocate funds effectively, prioritize investments, and monitor your financial performance. By creating and adhering to a comprehensive budget, you can ensure that your firm is on track to achieve its growth objectives while maintaining financial stability.

The first step in creating a budget for growth is to define your firm's financial goals. *What are your revenue targets? How much do you plan to invest in new hires, marketing, or technology?*

Once you've defined your goals, it's important to break them down into specific budget categories, such as salaries, marketing, office expenses, and technology investments. A firm that categorized their budget in this way found that it provided greater visibility into their spending, allowing them to identify areas where they could make adjustments or reallocate funds to support their priorities. For example, they were able to shift resources from non-essential office expenses to marketing, which helped drive client acquisition and revenue growth.

Budgeting for growth also requires you to anticipate and plan for potential challenges. This might include setting aside funds for unexpected expenses, such as legal fees or equipment repairs, as well as preparing for slower periods when revenue may be lower. By planning for the unexpected, firms are able to maintain momentum even when faced with unforeseen obstacles.

Finally, budgeting for growth requires a focus on return on investment (ROI). Every dollar spent should contribute to your firm's long-term success — whether it's through increased revenue, improved efficiency — or enhanced client satisfaction. Budgeting is a critical component of financial management and growth. By defining your financial goals, categorizing your budget, planning for challenges, monitoring performance, updating regularly, and focusing on ROI, you can create a budget that supports your firm's growth and ensures its long-term success.

Financial Reporting:
Gaining Insights and Driving Decisions
Regular financial reports provide insights into your firm's financial health, helping you make informed decisions and track your progress toward your financial goals. Here are a few critical reports to track as you grow and scale.

One of the most important financial reports for your firm is the profit and loss statement (P&L). This report provides a snapshot of your firm's profitability over a specific period, showing your revenue, expenses, and net income.

The balance sheet is another critical financial report. It provides a snapshot of your firm's financial position at a specific point in time, showing your assets, liabilities, and equity. A firm that regularly reviewed their balance sheet was able to maintain a strong financial position by ensuring that their assets exceeded their liabilities. This report also helped them manage their debt levels and ensure that they had the financial resources to support their growth.

Cash flow statements are also essential in helping you understand your firm's liquidity, ensuring that you have enough cash on hand to meet your obligations.

In addition to these core financial reports, it's important to track key performance indicators (KPIs) that are relevant to your firm's success. This might include metrics such as client acquisition cost, average revenue per client, or utilization rates. This allows you to make data-driven decisions that supported your current growth approach.

Regular financial reporting is essential for maintaining financial transparency and accountability within your firm. A firm that shared financial reports with their leadership team and key stakeholders found that it helped align everyone around their financial goals and supported more informed decision-making. This transparency also built trust within the firm, as everyone had a clear understanding of the firm's financial health and performance.

Financial reporting is a critical component of effective financial management. By ensuring accurate data, regularly reviewing key reports, tracking relevant KPIs, maintaining transparency, and using insights for continuous improvement, you can gain the insights you need to drive your firm's financial success and achieve your long-term goals.

Chapter 8 Key Takeaways

Jim Blake: Effective cash flow management is essential for maintaining financial stability and supporting growth, while a well-structured budget helps align your resources with your firm's strategic goals. Once these two areas are aligned, regular financial reporting provides the insights needed to make informed decisions, track progress, and drive continuous improvement.

By focusing on these three key areas, you can build a strong financial foundation that supports your firm's long-term success and growth.

Jason Navarro: Managing cash flow effectively is crucial for maintaining stability and enabling your firm to invest in its future. When you maste these aspects of financial management, you can create a firm that is not only profitable; but also resilient and well-positioned for long-term growth.

CHAPTER 9:
NAVIGATING CHALLENGES: ENSURING RESILIENCE AND ADAPTABILITY

Embracing Change: The Key to Long-Term Success

Whether it's evolving client needs, shifts in the regulatory landscape, or advances in technology, your firm's ability to adapt to change will determine its long-term success. Embracing change, in this case, isn't just about survival — it's about positioning your firm to thrive in a dynamic environment.

By fostering a culture of adaptability and resilience, you can ensure that your firm remains competitive and relevant, no matter what challenges come your way.

The first step in embracing change is to develop a proactive mindset. By staying informed and being proactive, your firm will be able to adapt their strategies and services to meet new demands, ensuring that they remained ahead of the curve.

Flexibility is also crucial when it comes to embracing change. Firms that are too rigid in their processes or resistant to new ideas often struggle to adapt when circumstances shift. A firm that cultivates a flexible approach to problem-solving and decision-making will find that it allows them to pivot quickly when needed — Whether the challenge is adopting new technology, adjusting service offerings, or exploring new markets.

As you might expect, leadership plays a key role in guiding your firm through periods of change. As a leader in the firm, it's your responsibility to set the tone for how your firm approaches change. This involves not only leading by example but also communicating the importance of adaptability to your team.

Finally, embracing change requires a willingness to take calculated risks. While it's important to carefully consider the potential outcomes of any decision, being overly cautious can sometimes prevent your firm from seizing new opportunities. A willingness to take calculated risks allows firms to stay ahead of the competition and drive growth.

Embracing change is essential for the long-term success of your firm. By developing a proactive mindset, cultivating flexibility, leading by example, investing in continuous learning, and taking calculated risks, you can ensure that your firm is well-positioned to navigate any challenge and seize new opportunities.

Managing Crisis: Strategies for Effective Response

Crises can and will occur, no matter how prepared your firm might be. Whether it's an economic downturn, a major client loss, or an internal disruption, the way you respond to a crisis can have a lasting impact on your firm's reputation and success.

Remember: Effective crisis management is about more than just damage control — it's about navigating the storm and emerging stronger on the other side.

The first step in managing a crisis is to have a plan in place. A firm that develops a comprehensive crisis management plan, outlining the steps to take in various scenarios, typically finds that it has a clear roadmap for action when and if a crisis occurs. This plan should include protocols for communication, decision-making, and resource allocation; ensuring that everyone knew their role and responsibilities during a crisis.

Firms that have this plan in place, are able to respond quickly and effectively, minimizing the impact of the crisis on their stakeholders.

Communication is critical during a crisis. Keeping your team, clients, and stakeholders informed about the situation and your firm's response is essential for maintaining trust and confidence. This level of communication can be done via email, phone calls, and meetings; ensuring that everyone was kept in the loop and knew what to expect.

Leadership is particularly important during times of crisis. As a leader, your team will look to you for guidance and reassurance. By remaining calm and composed, the leadership will set the tone for how the firm would navigate the crisis, fostering a sense of stability and resilience and, in a way, "predicting" a firm's resiliency and output as a result.

Flexibility and adaptability are also crucial when managing a crisis. No two crises are the same, and the ability to adjust your strategy as the situation evolves is essential.

Finally, after the crisis passes, it's time to learn and retain. Learning from the crisis is another important aspect of effective crisis management. After the immediate crisis has passed, conduct a thorough review of what happened, how it was handled, and what could be improved for the future.

Managing a crisis effectively requires preparation, communication, strong leadership, flexibility, and a commitment to learning from the experience. By focusing on these key elements, you can navigate crises successfully and ensure that your firm emerges stronger and more resilient.

Maintaining Client Trust During Difficult Times

During challenging periods, maintaining client trust is paramount. Whether your firm is facing a crisis, undergoing significant changes, or dealing with external challenges, how you communicate and manage client relationships during these times will determine the strength of your firm's reputation and client loyalty.

Transparency is the foundation of maintaining client trust during difficult times. Clients appreciate honesty, even when the news isn't positive.

Proactive communication is also essential. Rather than waiting for clients to reach out with concerns, many firms have found that clients appreciate a proactive approach to communication. This not only maintains trust, but also strengthens client relationships; as clients appreciated the firm's attentiveness and responsiveness.

Finally, showing appreciation for your clients' loyalty and understanding during difficult times can go a long way in maintaining trust. Whether it's through personalized notes, phone calls, or small tokens of appreciation, this gesture helps reinforce the firm's commitment to their clients and their appreciation for the trust that had been placed in them.

Maintaining client trust during difficult times requires transparency, proactive communication, empathy, delivering on promises, and showing appreciation. By focusing on these key elements, you can strengthen client relationships and ensure that your firm's reputation remains strong, even in the face of challenges.

Chapter 9 Key Takeaways

Jim Blake: Embracing change is essential for long-term success; it requires a proactive mindset, flexibility, and strong leadership to guide your firm through evolving circumstances.

This contributes to positive crisis management outcomes in which firms do more than just respond to immediate threats — instead maintaining communication, demonstrating strong leadership, and learning from the experience to emerge stronger.

Jason Navarro: During challenging times, maintaining client trust is key. This step can be achieved and maintained through transparency, proactive engagement, and a commitment to client satisfaction. By adopting these strategies, your firm will be well-equipped to handle any obstacle and continue growing stronger.

CHAPTER 10:
NETWORKING AND COLLABORATION: BUILDING RELATIONSHIPS FOR GROWTH

The Power of Networking

Networking allows you to build meaningful relationships that can lead to new opportunities, referrals, and collaborations. And, in the legal industry, where trust and reputation are paramount, your network can be one of your most valuable assets.

By strategically expanding your network and nurturing the relationships within it, you can create a strong foundation for long-term growth and success.

The first step in effective networking is to be intentional about the connections you make. Rather than attending every event or joining every organization, we recommend that you focus on those that align with your firm's goals and values. By targeting their networking efforts, firms are able to develop relationships with individuals who could directly contribute to their firm's growth.

Networking is successful once successful relationships are built. This means going beyond exchanging business cards or connecting on LinkedIn; taking time instead to get to know people — understanding their needs and finding ways to provide value.

Consistency is also important in networking. It's not enough to attend one event or send one email — you need to maintain regular contact with your network to keep the relationships strong. By staying in touch and nurturing relationships, firms are able to turn initial introductions into long-term professional connections.

Leveraging online platforms is another powerful way to expand your network. Social media, professional networking sites, and online forums provide opportunities to connect with a broader audience and engage with professionals outside of your immediate geographic area. Remember: Networking isn't just about what you can gain — it's also about what you can give. A firm that took a collaborative approach to networking, offering to share their expertise, provide introductions, or support others in their endeavors, found that it created a reciprocal environment where others were more likely to offer support in return. This collaborative mindset helped to build a network of contacts who were invested in each other's success, leading to more opportunities for referrals, partnerships, and growth.

Finally, measuring the effectiveness of your networking efforts is important to ensure that your time and resources are being well spent. A firm that regularly evaluated the impact of their networking activities, tracking the number of referrals, partnerships, and new clients generated through their network, was able to refine their strategy and focus on the most productive connections — and we'd love to see the same for you. Networking is a powerful tool for growth, but it requires a strategic and intentional approach. By being selective about the connections you make, and building authentic relationships, you can create a network that supports your firm's long-term success and growth.

Building Strategic Partnerships

Building strategic partnerships requires careful planning, clear communication, and a focus on mutual benefit. When done right, these partnerships can significantly contribute to your firm's growth and success.

The first step in building strategic partnerships is to identify potential partners who align with your firm's goals, values, and expertise. This might include other law firms, financial advisors, accountants, or even community organizations. Once you've identified potential partners, it's time to establish clear goals and expectations for the partnership. *What do you hope to achieve through this collaboration? How will you measure success?* Then, it's time to initiate and open the lines of communication. Regular, open communication helps to build trust, resolve issues, and ensure that both parties are on the same page.

As you network, consider measuring the success of your partnerships. This might involve tracking the number of referrals generated, the revenue impact of the partnership, or the overall satisfaction of both parties. this step allows you to refine your networking strategy, strengthen collaborations, and ensure that partnerships continued to deliver mutual value.

Strategic partnerships are a powerful way to expand your firm's reach and enhance the value you provide to your clients. By identifying the right partners, setting clear goals, maintaining open communication, focusing on collaboration, and measuring success, you can build partnerships that contribute to your firm's long-term growth and success.

The Role of Mentorship and Peer Relationships

Mentorship and peer relationships play a crucial role in professional development and firm growth. By learning from the experiences of others and building relationships with peers, you can gain valuable insights, develop new skills, and expand your network.

Providing mentorship is also a valuable way to give back and build your professional reputation. A firm that encouraged its attorneys to mentor younger professionals found that it not only helped to develop the next generation of legal talent, but also enhanced the firm's reputation as a leader in the field. By sharing their knowledge and experience, they were then able to build strong, lasting relationships that benefited both the mentors and the mentees.

Peer relationships are another important aspect of professional development. Engaging with your peers, whether through industry associations, networking groups, or online forums, allows you to exchange ideas, share experiences, and learn from each other. These peer relationships then create an organic support network to turn to for advice and collaboration.

Collaboration with peers can also lead to new opportunities for your firm. By working together with peers, firms are able to achieve more than they could on their own and create new opportunities for growth.

Like you would with other forms of networking, measuring the impact of mentorship and peer relationships is important — as it allows yourself and other stakeholders to understand and fully leverage their value.

Mentorship and peer relationships are powerful tools for professional development and firm growth. By seeking out mentorship, providing it, engaging with your peers, collaborating on opportunities, and measuring the impact of these relationships, you can gain valuable insights, expand your network, and drive your firm's success.

Collaborating with Other Firms: Expanding Your Reach

As mentioned, collaborating with other law firms can be a strategic way to expand your services, reach new markets, and enhance your firm's reputation. Below, we've listed the steps to help you launch a successful collaborative product. The first step in the collaborative process is to identify potential partners whose expertise and values align with your own. By choosing partners who complemented your practice areas, you can expand services and offer clients a more comprehensive legal solution.

Once you've identified potential partners, it's important to establish clear goals and expectations for the collaboration. *What do you hope to achieve through this partnership? How will you work together to provide the best possible service to your clients?*

Communication is critical in any collaboration. Regular, open communication helps to build trust, resolve issues, and ensure that both parties are on the same page. it also requires a focus on mutual benefit. By focusing on mutual benefits for themselves and for each other, firms are able to build strong, long-lasting collaborations that contribute to their firm's growth.

Measuring the success of your collaborations is also important. This might involve tracking the number of referrals generated, the revenue impact of the collaboration, or the overall satisfaction of both parties. This ultimately results in a firm's ability to refine its strategy, strengthen its partnerships, and ensure that its collaborations continue to deliver value.

Collaborating with other law firms is a powerful way to expand your reach and enhance the value you provide to your clients. By carefully selecting partners, setting clear goals, maintaining open communication, focusing on mutual benefit, and measuring success, you can create collaborations that contribute to your firm's long-term growth and success.

Chapter 10 Key Takeaways

Jim Blake: Effective networking is about building meaningful relationships that lead to new opportunities, referrals, and collaborations.

By being intentional in your networking efforts, building authentic relationships, and leveraging both in-person and online platforms, you can create a powerful network that supports your firm's growth.

Strategic partnerships, whether with other professionals or law firms, can significantly expand your services, reach new markets, and enhance the value you provide to your clients.

Mentorship and peer relationships are also vital for professional development and firm growth, offering valuable insights, support, and opportunities for collaboration.

Jason Navarro: Strategic partnerships allow you to collaborate with other professionals and firms to offer more comprehensive services and reach new markets. This collaboration can then be a strategic way to expand your services and enhance the value you provide to your clients. By embracing these strategies, you can create a strong network of relationships that support your firm's growth and ensure its long-term success.

CONCLUSION:
THE ROAD TO ACCELERATED GROWTH

We hope it's clear that building a million-dollar estate planning and elder law firm isn't just about implementing a few key strategies — it's about adopting an approach that touches every aspect of your practice. From the first spark of your vision to the daily operations that drive your firm forward, success is built on a foundation of strategic thinking, unwavering commitment, and continuous growth.

Throughout this book, we've explored the critical areas that contribute to your firm's success: strategic planning, branding, client acquisition, team building, financial management, and more. Each chapter has provided you with actionable insights and practical tools designed to empower you to take your firm to the next level.

But the journey doesn't end here.

Resilience and Adaptability: As discussed in Chapter 9, the ability to navigate challenges and adapt to change is crucial. The legal landscape is evolving, and your firm must be resilient enough to withstand external pressures and adaptable enough to seize new opportunities.

By embracing change, leading with confidence, and maintaining client trust, your firm can turn challenges into opportunities for growth.

The Power of Relationships: Chapter 10 highlighted the importance of networking and collaboration. Building strong, authentic relationships — whether with clients, colleagues, or strategic partners — can open doors to new opportunities and drive your firm's success. By investing in these relationships and approaching them with a mindset of mutual benefit, you can create a network that supports your long-term goals.

Financial Strength: As we explored in Chapter 8, a strong financial foundation is the bedrock of any successful firm. Sound financial management allows you to make informed decisions, invest in growth, and ensure that your firm remains profitable and sustainable. By mastering the principles of budgeting, cash flow management, and financial reporting, you can secure your firm's financial future.

Leadership and Vision: Leadership is the glue that holds all these elements together. Your ability to inspire, guide, and support your team is essential for creating a high-performance culture that drives your firm forward. By maintaining a clear vision and leading by example, you can steer your firm toward sustained success.

Continuous Improvement: Finally, the journey to building a million-dollar firm is one of continuous improvement. There's always room to refine your strategies, enhance your services, and better serve your clients. By committing to lifelong learning and staying open to new ideas, you can keep your firm on the path to unstoppable growth.

Your Next Steps: As you move forward, take a moment to reflect on the insights and strategies you've gained from this book. Identify the areas where your firm excels and where there's room for improvement. Set clear, actionable goals that align with your vision, and take the first steps toward achieving them.

Remember, success is not a destination—it's a journey. And with the right mindset, strategies, and support, you're well on your way to building the million-dollar firm you've always envisioned.

Here's to your continued success and the unstoppable growth of your practice.

To your success,
Jim Blake & Jason Navarro

ABOUT BAMBIZ

At Bambiz, we understand the unique challenges estate planning and elder law attorneys face — and we're here to help you navigate them with confidence. Since 2016, we've been partnering with firms just like yours; providing innovative marketing strategies, cutting-edge technology, and hands-on guidance to help you achieve real growth.

We believe that building a successful, future-ready law firm requires more than just marketing — it's about creating a lasting connection with your community, building trust with your clients, and staying ahead of the curve with modern strategies.

That's why we offer:

- **Targeted Digital Marketing:** Whether it's social media management or high-converting ad campaigns, we help you attract the right clients and establish meaningful relationships.

- **Lead Generation Tools:** From webinars to seminars, we design and run powerful campaigns that consistently bring in qualified leads and consultations.

- **Custom Websites and SEO:** We craft tailored, high-performing websites optimized to rank in search engines and attract local clients who are actively searching for your services.

- **Workshops and Educational Events:** Our workshops and seminars are a cornerstone of what we do. Known for delivering actionable insights, these events give attorneys the tools and knowledge they need to grow their practices and stay competitive.

- **Client Engagement and Retention:** We equip you with the right tools to keep your clients engaged and loyal, from effective email newsletters to reputation management strategies.

As you'll see, we don't just offer services at Bambiz — we build lasting partnerships. Our team is proud to work closely with you to create a customized marketing strategy that fits your firm's specific goals and challenges.

Together, we'll help you grow your practice, reach new clients, and ensure long-term success.

Ready to Learn More?

Visit www.bambiz.net to dive deeper into our services, explore success stories from other firms, and find out about our upcoming events. We'd love to talk about how we can partner with you to grow your practice and help you build the future-ready law firm you've always envisioned.

ABOUT THE AUTHORS

Jim Blake, founder and CEO of Bambiz, is dedicated to helping law firms grow using modern, results-driven marketing strategies. With a deep understanding of the unique challenges estate planning and elder law attorneys face, Jim has developed systems that consistently deliver measurable success. He's also the author of multiple books on growth for law firms, sharing proven strategies that have helped countless firms build practices that hit seven figures and beyond.

Jason Navarro leads the growth department at Bambiz, where he brings a deep expertise in strategic planning and scaling businesses. His focus is on helping attorneys put systems in place that not only drive growth but also give them back time to focus on their clients and firm. Jason's approach to business development has been key in shaping the hands-on, client-centered strategies that Bambiz offers.

Additional Resources for Success

As you continue on the journey to transform your estate planning and elder law firm into a million-dollar practice, leveraging the right resources can significantly accelerate your success. Below are comprehensive tools, organizations, and learning platforms that will support your growth and help you implement the strategies discussed in this book.

1. Marketing and Client Acquisition: Bambiz

Of course, we wrote this book, so we're a little biased, but…

…when it comes to marketing and client acquisition for elder law and estate planning attorneys, **Bambiz** is your go-to partner.

We specialize in creating tailored marketing solutions that not only get you noticed but also help you build lasting relationships with your clients. Offering content creation, comprehensive marketing strategies, 1:1 support, and more; our services are designed to attract and retain the clients you want.

Reach out today — whether you're looking to fill your next workshop or just need a fresh approach to digital marketing, we've got your back! Website: **www.bambiz.net**

2. Professional Organizations

Joining professional organizations allows your firm to enjoy invaluable networking opportunities, access to industry research, and continuing education resources. Consider becoming a member of:

- **American Bar Association (ABA):** The ABA offers a vast array of resources for legal professionals, including specialized publications, webinars, and networking events. Their sections on real property, trust, and estate law are particularly beneficial for estate planning attorneys looking to deepen their expertise.

- **Lawyers with Purpose:** Lawyers with Purpose provides estate planning and elder law attorneys with systems, software, and support to run their practices efficiently. Membership includes access to a community of like-minded professionals and resources tailored to estate planning and elder law.

- **National Academy of Elder Law Attorneys (NAELA):** NAELA provides a wealth of resources tailored to elder law professionals, including educational programs, networking opportunities, and updates on legislative changes that can impact your practice. Being part of NAELA connects you with a community dedicated to excellence in elder law.

- **State Bar Associations:** Local bar associations often provide resources specific to estate planning and elder law, including practice guides, CLE opportunities, and networking events. Engaging with your state bar can help you connect with other professionals and stay informed about local legal developments.

- **WealthCounsel:** WealthCounsel offers comprehensive legal education and practice support for attorneys specializing in estate planning and elder law. Membership includes access to a vast library of resources, forms, and tools.

3. Online Learning Platforms

Investing in your professional development is crucial for staying ahead in a competitive market. Online learning platforms offer courses that can enhance your knowledge in areas relevant to your practice:

- **Coursera:** Coursera partners with top universities and organizations, allowing them to offer courses on legal topics, business management, and marketing strategies. We recommend that you look for courses on estate planning, elder law, and legal technology to sharpen your skills.

- **Lawline:** Specializing in on-demand CLE courses for attorneys, Lawline offers content on ethics, practice management, and emerging trends in estate planning and elder law. These courses are designed to keep you updated on the latest developments in the field.

- **LinkedIn Learning:** LinkedIn Learning provides a comprehensive library of courses that supplements your ongoing training in law practice management, client relations, and digital marketing. Consider exploring courses on building a client-centric practice or mastering legal technology tools to boost your firm's efficiency.

4. Books and Publications

Enhance your knowledge and refine your practice management, marketing, and financial strategies by exploring these essential books:

- **"Unstoppable Growth" by Jim Blake:** Jim Blake's *Unstoppable Growth* provides a strategic approach to scaling your firm, emphasizing empowerment, client-centric success, and the mindset required to achieve long-term growth.

- **"Building a StoryBrand" by Donald Miller:** This book offers a clear framework for clarifying your message and creating marketing that connects with your audience, helping you build a brand that resonates with clients.

- **"The E-Myth Attorney" by Michael E. Gerber:** This book emphasizes the importance of building systems and processes within your law practice, helping you focus on growing your business rather than just working in it.

- **"The Trusted Advisor" by David H. Maister:** Focusing on the importance of building trust with clients, this book provides strategies for becoming a trusted advisor — a key component of client retention and referrals.

- **"Profit First" by Mike Michalowicz:** Michalowicz's approach to financial management prioritizes profitability by encouraging business owners to allocate profits first. This book offers actionable steps to improve your firm's financial health.

5. Technology Tools

The right technology can streamline operations and enhance client service, making your firm more competitive. We've given you a few starting points below:

- **Clio:** This tool is a leading practice management software for law firms; offering features for case management, billing, and client communication. Its user-friendly interface and robust tools help you manage your practice more efficiently.

- **DecisionVault:** DecisionVault is an intake portal designed for estate planning practices. It streamlines the client intake process by centralizing and automating data collection.

- **DocuSign:** This electronic signature solution simplifies the signing process for legal documents, enhancing client convenience and speeding up agreement execution. It's particularly useful for estate planning documents that require multiple signatures.

- **Estateably:** Estateably provides estate and trust administration software designed for legal professionals. It offers features like document automation, accounting, and task management.

- **LEAP:** LEAP provides comprehensive estate planning and probate software tailored for attorneys; offering features such as document automation, legal accounting, time tracking, case management, and secure document sharing.

- **Zoom:** With remote consultations becoming more common, Zoom is now an essential for virtual client meetings. Its screen-sharing and recording features can improve client interactions and make communication more effective.

6. Mentorship and Coaching

Seeking mentorship or coaching from experienced professionals in the legal field can provide invaluable guidance as you grow your practice. Our recommended sources include:

- **Atticus Advantage:** Atticus Advantage offers business coaching, practice management systems, and resources specifically designed for lawyers. Their programs focus on increasing profitability, improving work-life balance, and building a sustainable law practice.

- **Hiring and Empowering Solutions:** This program focuses on transforming legal teams into efficient, resourceful, and profitable assets through leadership development.

- **New Law Business Model (NLBM):** NLBM offers coaching, business systems, and support for lawyers; focusing on Life & Legacy Planning to build a successful law practice.

- **2-Hour Lifestyle Lawyer:** Helps attorneys establish and market a profitable estate planning practice with minimal work hours.

7. Networking Opportunities

Engaging with peers in your field can provide new insights and foster collaboration. Here are a few places to consider exploring:

- **Industry Conferences and Workshops:** We recommend that you attend events to connect with other professionals and learn about best practices and emerging trends in estate planning and elder law.

- **Local Networking Events:** Additionally, participating in local events helps you build relationships within your community and expand your referral network.

- **Online Forums and Discussion Groups:** Lastly, consider engaging in online communities to share knowledge, discuss challenges, and stay informed about industry developments.

Take Your Growth to the Next Level

It's time to put these strategies into action and supercharge your results!

We've created exclusive bonus materials to give you an extra edge. By scanning the QR code below, you'll unlock access to advanced growth tactics, marketing tools, and in-depth video tutorials.

These resources are updated regularly, ensuring you have the latest tools and strategies to continue scaling your practice.

https://bambiz.net/accelerated-growth-bonus

www.ingramcontent.com/pod-product-compliance
Lightning Source LLC
Chambersburg PA
CBHW052303220526
45471CB00001B/463